Watch Hill Style

Richard C. Youngken
In collaboration with Chaplin B. Barnes

Watch Hill Style

Table of Contents

Preface   5

Watch Hill Style   9
   Doorways & Entrances   11
   Roofs   15
   Porches & Loggias   19
   Windows   23
   Textures   27
   Landscapes & Gardens   31
   Architectural Compositions   34

Architects & Designers...   39
   ...Some of Their Work at Watch Hill   41

Landscape Architects & Their Work   49

Glossary   52

References with Select Annotations   54

Acknowledgements

The Watch Hill Conservancy gratefully acknowledges the many Watch Hill "cottage" owners who have supported this project, welcoming us to their homes and permitting us to use the photographic images captured. A similar generosity on the part of the various Watch Hill non-profit organizations provided valuable access to their resources, including their archives. Both Joan Youngken and Barbara T. Barnes provided valuable proofreading, editing, and format suggestions. Finally, we express our deep appreciation to The Alfred M. Roberts, Jr. Charitable Foundation, whose generous support made this enterprise possible.

The Watch Hill Conservancy
Copyright 2009
ISBN 0-9770586-1-1

Preface

Watch Hill, Rhode Island's distinctive late 19th- and early 20th-century summer colony architecture and its surviving integrity have earned it a listing in the National Register of Historic Places maintained by the Department of the Interior. This is the nation's list of buildings, sites, and districts that are significant for their contribution to our American heritage, their state of preservation, and their ability to convey the American experience with considerable authenticity.

The development of Watch Hill's private summer homes followed an era when large post-Civil War resort hotels had dominated the landscape of this point of land framed with water on three sides. It was during that earlier period that the health-restoring, recreational aspects of Watch Hill's somewhat isolated seaside location were discovered by urban families of means who sought a summer escape from the heat, noise, grime, confusion, and density of city life. Here they found a respite close to nature with the cooling and restorative aspects of the Atlantic Ocean at hand. Many of Watch Hill's summer visitors came not just from the cities of the Eastern seaboard but also from the Midwest, the earliest of the cottagers from Cincinnati, Ohio.

Families returned each summer, later participating in a shift to summer cottage building as the hotel venues generally lost appeal toward the end of the 19th century and as surrounding farmland became available for development. Their new cottages, together with private clubs – golf, tennis, yacht, and beach – became the new focus of social life.

This shift from hotels to cottages was not unique to Watch Hill. It also occurred at other Northeast seaside resorts, among them, in Rhode Island, those at Narragansett, Jamestown, and Newport. At Watch Hill, the wave of house building followed the initial land investment in the early 1880s of a Cincinnati-based syndicate of summer visitors who saw the appeal that private summer residences would offer over communal and more formal hotel life, bought farmland adjacent to the hotel area, and sold lots to friends and fellow summer visitors.

The large collection of summer houses that comprise most of the Watch Hill Historic District were built over the relatively short span of twenty years, roughly between 1886 and 1906, within an expanding curvilinear street pattern inspired by the designs of landscape architect Frederick Law Olmsted, Sr. These "cottages," as they were called, were designed and built in compatible summer house architecture popular at the time and are, as a result, rather homogeneous in character. They are a window into the taste and style of those of the period who were successful in their businesses and professions, and could afford an extended and relaxing vacation – at a time when American enterprise and audacity were gaining the world's attention.

Accomplished architects, designers, and builders were employed to create Watch Hill's cottages. In the brief time period in which most of these cottages were built, architectural interest and taste in the northeastern states centered primarily on evolving wood-framed and shingled American interpretations of earlier post-medieval, colonial, and craftsman building forms and embellishments, the result of which were the Shingle Style, Colonial Revival, and the American Arts and Crafts movements. Much of the summer residential architecture of Watch Hill is a *blend* of these three artistic trends into a distinctive and iconic *Watch Hill Style*. The "cottage colony," as the Watch Hill summer community became known, was later embellished with an eclectic mix of cottages in the Norman, Tudor, and Mediterranean revival styles, all of which share with the earlier structures a relaxed and organic architectural connection.

What was true more than a quarter century ago (1985), when Watch Hill was listed in the National Register, is still true today, as stated in the nomination: Watch Hill's "...country-house architecture for the well-to-do represented the epitome of good taste.... Watch Hill is a remarkably well-preserved historical community notable for its architectural and environmental quality and its evocation of an important phase in American social history."

Watch Hill's preservation is no accident. The colony and its cottages have retained their draw among the families who have summered here over generations. Many of the cottages today are still owned by descendants of the early cottagers or those related through marriage and kinship. This continuity of community, which Chaplin Barnes chronicles in *Watch Hill Through Time*, has led to continued interest in Watch Hill's architectural resources, their setting, and their preservation, and has in turn attracted new families to settle here.

While the Watch Hill Historic District is listed in the National Register, this Federal designation carries no *local* design review authority. However, at the instigation of the Watch Hill Conservancy, the Town of Westerly has adopted design review standards for the Village commercial area. Westerly Town Charter revisions in 2008 provide for the establishment of a town-wide architectural review board, and the Rhode Island Coastal Resources Management Council (CRMC) is required to seek opinions from the Rhode Island Historical Preservation and Heritage Commission (RIHPHC) regarding the impacts of coastal projects. These initiatives indicate a growing community sentiment that design review can be extremely beneficial in preserving the character of a place. Absent specific

design review regulations for Watch Hill's cottages, however, an awareness of the design elements which contribute to their special character can go far to encourage compatible new construction when it is contemplated.

The goal of this modest primer on Watch Hill's historic architectural style is to provide a guide for those considering new construction or preservation, to assist in understanding, appreciating, and respecting the colony's architectural heritage and character.

While not all new construction at Watch Hill has enhanced the Historic District, and in recent years a number of historic cottages have been lost through demolition or misguided renovations, much new construction complements the Historic District, demonstrating that finely wrought, context-sensitive design blends in rather than detracts. A few images showing elements of this recent work are included in this book together with those of the historic architecture. In much of this successful new building, historic design details are carefully interplayed and subtly reinterpreted with *restraint* in the *right proportion and detail*, to create new and interesting compositions that add to Watch Hill's architectural charm.

Not shown is the new construction in Watch Hill that has not been as sensitive as it might have been. Here features such as mannerist or out-of-scale building elements, super-sized massing, and large window openings have created an incongruous effect. But this is the exception, rather than the rule.

The Watch Hill Conservancy, whose mission includes the preservation of the natural and built environments of Watch Hill and the conservation, maintenance, and enhancement of its historical values and character, has commissioned this introduction to the architecture of Watch Hill in the hope that it will inspire continued stewardship of Watch Hill's architectural resources.

Watch Hill Style

Watch Hill stands apart in the minds of many as a unique place on the New England coast. But what makes Watch Hill so remarkable? Its natural beauty, of course, is striking, but Watch Hill has also evolved architecturally to complement that beauty.

Developed as a small residential summer enclave and remaining relatively intact for over a century, Watch Hill is defined by its location on a coastal peninsula, its rolling topography, protected harbor, miles of soft, white, sandy beaches, and architecturally significant 19th- and early 20th-century summer houses. The Watch Hill style exemplified in these large Shingle, early Craftsman, Colonial Revival, and academic revival-styled summer houses is relaxed and simple, centered on the weather, time of day, and the pastimes of summer on the New England coast: gardening, tennis, fishing, sailing, golf, entertaining, and enjoying the beach. The architecture and the surrounding landscape provide the stage set for this leisurely lifestyle. As a result, the cottage colony of Watch Hill is an icon of the New England summer.

What, then, is Watch Hill's architectural essence? By exploring individual design elements – doorways, roofs, porches, windows, textures, and materials, and their use – one can begin to understand the component pieces of what makes Watch Hill architecture so visually engaging. These elements from the popular styles of the period are combined in summer house architecture to enable the owners to enjoy family, guests, and a vital connection to the outdoors. Wide, furnished porches, both open and enclosed, provide indoor-outdoor living spaces cooled by ocean breezes. Large, open rooms are often painted white and furnished in sea-inspired colors. These spaces often flow from a large central "living hall," an innovation introduced with the Queen Anne and Shingle Style architecture of the period. Second and third stories full of bedrooms bring the family together, although, at the time of construction, the top floor was generally the realm of servants. Popular architectural details are often combined – Queen Anne flourishes, Shingle Style stone foundations with shingled walls, Colonial Revival entrances and windows, Craftsman eaves, and exposed rafters. Everything is comfortable, spacious, and understated. The elements are used with restraint and a sense of proportion.

The "cottage" label given to these summer houses is more reflective of an informal and carefree lifestyle, with comfortable interiors, than descriptive of size or pretention. Most of the cottages appear larger than they actually are. Many are just one room wide. The architecture and its landscaped setting fit together in comfortable unity. One of the remarkable features of Watch Hill is that it has survived as an architectural and social ensemble. It endures because it is appreciated and well-loved, embodying time-honored traditions, and a sense of place and permanence.

Doorways & Entrances

Much of the character of these cottages is pronounced in their entrances. Some are more imposing than others, but in general front doorways are downplayed to create a sense of summer informality, especially considering the scale of each house. Often the front door is set within a porch; many are within symmetrical Colonial Revival frames with pilasters, cornices, fanlights, and sidelights. The doors themselves are often Dutch Colonial double doors that can be half-opened as a welcome greeting to arriving guests. These doorways are notably consistent regardless of the overall form of the house.

Meticulously groomed privet hedges have now become a Watch Hill signature, many having arched openings and distinctive gates to welcome visitors arriving by foot or bicycle, leading them by a pathway to the house.

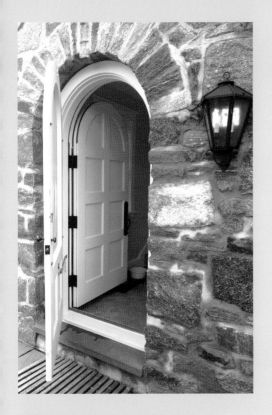

Roofs

Texture and form are the bywords for Watch Hill's roofs. Many are complex arrangements of gables, hips, upswept roof lines, projecting eaves, and dormers. Some are quite symmetrical, mounding up like a layer cake, while others ramble and elongate after rising from the first floor to shelter multi-story cottages. Many roofs are still wood-shingled. They are part and parcel of the Shingle Style and early Craftsman houses they adorn with their wide-bracketed eaves or exposed rafter ends, and gabled, hipped, or shed-roofed dormers. In the sea-air climate, these roofs weather after only one season. Some roofs are slate, resembling medieval stone roofs and adding to the architectural character of the Norman and Tudor Revival cottages they shelter. There are some red clay tile roofs as well, providing a distinctive look to several Spanish, Moorish, or Mission-inspired houses. There is even one whose wood shingles whimsically mimic English cottage thatch. The variety of chimneys is also notable.

Porches & Loggias

Watch Hill's porches are wide and generous, often designed as a transition to the garden and framing views to the sea. Here families enjoy all-weather summer activities: reading, napping, cocktails, and dining. On hot days these porches capture the sea breezes and on rainy days they provide shelter. Porch columns are often Tuscan or gothic-arched in a Craftsman style; some have a certain whimsy and playfulness. Many porches are partially enclosed with multiple windows in light, transparent arrangements which help retain an open and rustic porch feel. Some porches have an end wall of glass doors as a shield against the prevailing southwest wind. Some have been converted to sunrooms with multi-paned, inward-opening casements or sliding multi-paned windows. In some cases the windows slide down into a boxed, shingled balustrade underneath, vanishing from sight when open. In a few cottages, interior rooms have a sunroom feel and may connect directly to outdoor spaces.

Windows

Most windows in Watch Hill, large or small, are multi-paned, giving special character to the cottages with their wooden muntin bars and frames. Some windows display diagonal muntin bar patterns in a medieval style. Some give a stern-gallery nautical appearance. Configurations include fanlights, projecting bays, and glazed multi-paned French doors opening to porches. Larger windows are often framed in decorative ways with ornamental muntin configurations in Craftsman motifs adding a bit of whimsy.

Some windows from the earliest period of Watch Hill's cottage development are round-headed and framed by decorative gable bargeboards or bracket work.

Textures

Watch Hill's distinctive architecture is richly textured, from cobblestone foundations to shingled walls and roofs.

Texture is a driving characteristic of cottage exterior design. Many cottages are shingled with either red or white cedar. Red tends to darken over time; white may turn silver gray. The late 19th-century Shingle Style derives its name from such buildings, their idiosyncratic forms sheathed tightly in shingle work, some of which is decorative and patterned.

Other cottages from the same period, but of a more medieval revival style and Norman or Tudor derivation, are of solid stone or brick masonry appearance. Some are "half-timbered" with exposed wood framing systems or decorative work. Some are stuccoed or parged to resemble whitewashed stone. These houses bear a similarity to the English Craftsman traditions popular in suburban Britain and America at the time of their construction.

Landscapes & Gardens

The roadways and lanes of Watch Hill are bordered by hedges, fences, and cobblestone walls to the degree that some of the cottages are barely visible and glimpsed only through small garden gates or from driveway entrances. This was not always the case. In the late 19th and early 20th centuries, the landscape was much more open and there were few hedges. As the summer colony evolved and more privacy was sought, property borders along the roads were planted with the ubiquitous hedging seen today. These hedges are now very much a part of the heritage and character of the area.

A number of cottages have simple perennial borders along their hedges. Some have defined cottage gardens, cutting gardens, rose gardens, or a fenced potager. Driveways are often gravel-surfaced with brick or Belgian block entrances; those with driveway circles or forecourts may have a porte-cochere, or a level entrance from the drive to the house. Terraces around the cottages are often stone; otherwise the cottage may have a wood-framed porch entrance from the front walk or drive. Whether terrace or porch, most are decorated with pots of annuals. Garages are rarely visible, nor are automobiles prominently in view. Similarly the modern deck or system of decks is not widespread.

While the spread of vegetation has transformed Watch Hill's landscape from open fields to zones of cover and privacy, the cottagers are zealously protective of their views to the water and this vital link to a seaside location and identity. By longstanding tradition they try to position and maintain their plantings to protect the views of neighbors. This same sensitivity and intuitive response to place influences decisions or concerns as to the siting of new houses and additions.

Architectural Compositions

Watch Hill doorways, entrances, roofs, porches, windows, and wall surfaces combine within design configurations in half a dozen or so distinctive architectural compositions or ensembles with due care given to the right proportion, rhythm of window and door openings, roof line, and other details. The scale and massing of the buildings and their relationship to their settings is equally important. Although landscaping now shields some cottages from view, many are in close proximity to each other, necessitating sensitivity and care with these elements of composition.

For Watch Hill's Shingle, Colonial Revival, and early Craftsman Style cottages, descriptive labels are helpful to distinguish one cottage form from another. Important keys to identification are the roof type, footprint, and massing of the house.

Hip-Roofed Block

The basic hip-roofed block massing, usually in a two-story configuration and even in those of three or more stories, is used to create considerable volume. These cottages are generally large, shingled houses with Colonial Revival symmetry, with floor plans at least two rooms wide, front to back. The massing and architectural details create a vertical, layered look. Often upper-level balustrades, roof decks, and recently-added widows' walks add to the verticality. Generally these houses have shed- or hip-roofed dormers to accent their hipped roofs as well as exposed rafter ends under their roof soffits.

Cross Gable

The cross-gable form allows for more asymmetry and less formality of design than the hip-roofed block form. These cottages are generally more in the Shingle Style, with Colonial Revival details. Some of the more recently-built cottages in this form may display more ornamentation than the earlier ones in decorative gable-end bracket work, stylistically a hold-over or re-interpretation of the earlier High Victorian Gothic and Queen Anne styles.

High Gable

The simple end-gable form is a dominant feature reminiscent of chalets in the mountainous regions of Europe. By the late 19th century, the chalet had been popularized in earlier and contemporary architectural pattern books for vacation cottages. The high gable is also a throwback to the 17th-century post-medieval forms of early American houses, gaining popularity after the nation's bicentennial celebration in 1876, after which a nostalgia for all things "Colonial" held sway.

Double Gable

The double-gable form in the Shingle and English Tudor Revival styles popular at the turn of the century harkens to a romantically-inspired look at medieval sources, including the half-timbered, double-gabled English cottage.

This form advanced through the Shingle Style to more detailed double-gabled medieval revival houses in the early 20th century, made popular with the more refined architecture of the English Arts and Crafts style. The double gable also has become popular in late 20th-century Shingle Style revival architecture at Watch Hill.

Flanking Wings

These cottages are among the largest in Watch Hill, carrying in their form a Georgian formality and also harkening back to the medieval H-shaped plan found in many English country houses.

Splayed Wings

Often these cottages are just one room deep from back to front and seem much larger than they actually are, rambling along a ridge or promontory. Usually two-and-a-half stories in height, they have a central core with wings angled inward to define a front circle or entry court. These cottages convey their Craftsman inspiration with details such as diamond-patterned windows and exposed rafter ends. They are usually hip-roofed with shed- or hip-roofed dormers.

Gable on Gable

Shingle Style cottages often convey the most complex massing in a disarmingly subtle way. Roof gables are not always of equal size, and their juxtaposition allows for second and third stories to be enclosed within the roof. Expressed with a skin of shingles stretched across the frame of a building, wrapping under the eaves, and with a minimum of ornamentation, this cottage form embodies the Shingle Style. Here the great intersecting roof gables give volume for the second and third floors and are reminiscent of the austerity of the 17th-century gable-roofed post-medieval houses of our Colonial forebears.

Gable with Turret

The shingled turret form is carried through from the Queen Anne Style, usually as an extension of the porch on the first level. Often the turret has been enclosed.

Gambrel

Adopted by Shingle Style architects, the gambrel roof form evokes nostalgia for the simple vernacular American New England and Dutch Colonial houses of the 18th century and also provides considerable space for bedrooms under the eaves in a second and sometimes third floor or garret. Often referred to as "Modern Colonial," this form is frequently seen at Watch Hill, sometimes enlivened with cross gambrels or gambrel-roofed dormers.

Other Forms

Watch Hill's shingled cottage architecture evolved in the early 20th century to larger imposing revival versions of European country house styles. Cottages in the Norman, Tudor, and Mediterranean revival styles were built on large parcels further removed from the harbor and the Village. A Bermuda-style cottage from the 1950s adds another unexpected element. While strikingly different, these cottages nevertheless blend in with the Shingle Style, Craftsman, and Colonial Revival work of the late 19th century, and add a pleasing variety and romance to Watch Hill's architectural character.

Architects & Designers...

A number of Watch Hill's cottages are known to have been designed by noteworthy regional and national architects whose work likely influenced the design of many other buildings in the National Register district. Many of these designers were of the first generation of Americans to receive a formal education in architecture. Among them were George Keller, Edward Foote Hinkle, Henry W. Wilkinson, Albert Winslow Cobb, Grosvenor Atterbury, John A. Tompkins II, Horace S. Frazer, H. Van Buren Magonigle, Evarts Tracy, William Ralph Emerson, Wilson Eyre, John Russell Pope, Warrington Lawrence, and Mott B. Schmidt. Well-known landscape architects, the Olmsted Brothers, Warren Manning, Wadley and Smythe, and Marian Cruger Coffin, were also involved in creating a few of Watch Hill's garden and park landscapes.

Providing a stunning collection, the work of these noted designers at Watch Hill, represented in over three dozen cottages and their gardens, interprets the taste of the late 19th and early 20th centuries and embodies the timeless search for honest materials and craftsmanship. The architects and landscape architects who practiced at Watch Hill represent the very best

design talent of their time, ranking with such of their mentors and colleagues (with whom they trained or collaborated) as Peabody and Stearns; McKim, Mead and White; Gustav Stickley; Delano and Aldrich; Carrere and Hastings; and Frederick Law Olmsted, Sr. Lesser known architects are also represented including, John Cherry; Gardner, Pyne and Gardner; and E.F. Gilbert. The architectural forms at Watch Hill are generally reminiscent of much earlier buildings, both in the colonial Americas and in medieval Europe, where fine handwork and craftsmanship in natural building materials were the norm. Much of the work is in the Shingle Style, Colonial Revival, and early Craftsman styles, ubiquitous along the New England coast. The cottages convey artistic experimentation and a blending of these design interests of the period.

The popularity of the Shingle Style and the American Arts and Crafts movement lasted from the early 1880s to the First World War. The Shingle Style was the refined building style for those who had the confidence to embrace a truly American architectural form. It was particularly attractive for the relaxed lifestyle of a carefree summer vacation. Summer cottages such as those at Watch Hill have been described as "mansions in informal summer attire." Following the romantic period of the Victorian era, these buildings reflect the past in art and architecture and convey a sense of whimsy and delight in the unexpected. Whimsy is a fundamental part of the Watch Hill Style.

The summer cottages designed and built along the New England coast were highlighted in contemporary periodicals. Pattern books, such as those by John Calvin Stevens and Albert Winslow Cobb (above), and Gustav Stickley, among others, also celebrated the look and provided inspiration. Undoubtedly such resources inspired Watch Hill's cottagers and their designers in building their summer homes.

The Timbers, 1917,
designed by John Russell Pope

...Some of Their Work at Watch Hill

Keller

George Keller, Hartford, Connecticut (1842-1935)

A prominent Irish-born Hartford architect, Keller is responsible for a vast collection of buildings and structures - churches, houses, public buildings, and memorials - throughout the Hartford area and the region. He trained in the offices of Charles F. Anderson, the Washington, D.C. architect of the Senate and House wings of the National Capitol prior to the Civil War, and moved to Hartford in 1864. Keller's association with Watch Hill is the result of the patronage of James L. Howard, a manufacturer of railroad car parts and a summer resident of Watch Hill, a founder of the Watch Hill Chapel Society, and Lieutenant Governor of Connecticut in the late 1880s.

Keller's architectural work, including the interior of the *Watch Hill Chapel*, emphasizes High Victorian Gothic forms and decoration inspired by the enormously influential 19th-century British art critic John Ruskin. Through his work, Keller espoused a belief in honesty of materials and the picturesque which the romantic Gothic styles conveyed. Often these forms are vertical, expressed in high towers and steep roofs. Keller was not fond of pretense or the Classical Revival. Although his work is not of the Stick Style, which was popular elsewhere as a prelude to the Queen Anne and Shingle Styles, his Watch Hill work, shown on this page, is a bridge between the early mansard-roofed hotels and the shingled cottages.

By-The-Sea, 1879

Collins Cottage, 1880

Seaswept (Ocean Mound), ca.1880

Watch Hill Chapel, 1876-1902

Wilkinson

Henry Wilhelm Wilkinson, Syracuse and New York (1870-1931)

The son of a Syracuse, N.Y. banker, Wilkinson studied architecture at Cornell University under architect-professor and Gothicist Charles Babcock. After graduating in 1890, he worked for Cram, Goodhue and Ferguson, the celebrated Boston-based firm of Ralph Adams Cram, a fellow medievalist and noted Gothic Revival architect. While in Boston, Wilkinson was a founding member of the Arts and Crafts Society. Returning to Syracuse by 1900, he joined with Gustav Stickley to create the initial American Craftsman movement, combining influences of the English Arts and Crafts style made popular by such architects and designers as William Morris, Philip Webb, Richard Norman Shaw, and later Voysey, Scott, and Mackintosh. Wilkinson designed furniture for Stickley and at least one of his house plans was published in *The Craftsman* magazine. Moving to New York City, he embarked upon an architectural career of his own after 1903. His Watch Hill commissions at the turn of the century coincide with a formative period in his work, presumably while he was working with Cram in Boston and during his early career with Stickley.

Hinkle

Edward Foote Hinkle, New York (1876-?)

Hinkle, a member of a prominent Cincinnati family, attended Andover and Yale, graduating in 1901. Thereafter, he attended Cambridge University and the Ecole des Beaux-Arts, completing his studies in architecture and design from 1901-1905, and returning to receive a number of Watch Hill commissions on Lighthouse Point from the Clement A. Griscom family in 1906 and 1907. He built *Aktaion* (later *Moana*) for himself on land given to him by the Griscoms. Others shown here are *The Point, Trespasso,* and *Edgewater.*

Taurento, 1907, is shown on page 11, top right and on page 50. Not shown is *Napatree,* ca.1907 (not extant).

Neowam, 1900

Edgemere, built 1886, enlarged 189

Wetumanetu, 1899

Graydon, 190

The Point (The Manor House), 190

Moana (Aktaion), 1906

Edgewater (Edgecliff), 1907

Trespasso, 190

Atterbury and Tompkins

Grosvenor Atterbury, New York (1869-1956)

Born in Detroit, educated at Yale, Columbia's Graduate School of Architecture, and the Ecole des Beaux-Arts, Atterbury initially worked in the offices of McKim, Mead and White before partnering with John Tompkins in the late 1890s. Atterbury is known for his restoration designs for New York City Hall (1902), the model Forest Hills Garden planned residential community in Queens, and numerous seaside and country houses throughout the country, notably on Long Island's North Shore. Atterbury's work was published widely, including by Gustav Stickley in *The Craftsman* (1908).

John Almy Tompkins II, New York (1871-1941)

Born in Baltimore and educated at St. Paul's School and Columbia, Tompkins traveled extensively in Great Britain and Europe from 1894 until his association with Atterbury and their Forest Hills Gardens commission. Tompkins is credited with many of the Watch Hill commissions of the Atterbury and Tompkins partnership. Tompkins' patron in Watch Hill was Mrs. Clara Hunter Stanton of New York, who commissioned designs for five cottages between 1899 and her death in 1914 *(Tepee, Wigwam, The Wickiup, The Bungalow* and *Marbella)*.

Tepee *(Montrose)*, 1899, is shown on page 17, top right. Not shown are: *Marbella (Chenowith, The Ledges)*, ca.1914 (not extant); *Wigwam (Rosemont, Redlac)*, 1900 (attributed to Tompkins).

The Bungalow, 1899

High Wicket (Sowanniu, Chuckle Hill, Greyside North), 1900

The Knoll (The Folly), 1899

The Wickiup, 1900 (attributed to Tompkins)

Sunset Hill, 1915

The Misquamicut Club, 1900-1919

Tracy and Magonigle

Evarts Tracy, New York (1869-1929)

Tracy graduated from Yale in 1890, attended the Ecole des Beaux-Arts, and worked in the offices of McKim, Mead and White. He was in association briefly with Magonigle in the mid-late 1890s while the partnership's Watch Hill work was underway.

Harold van Buren Magonigle, New York (1867-1935)

Unlike many of his colleagues, Magonigle did not receive a formal education in architecture, but he did acquire extensive on-the-job training with a number of important architectural firms including Calvert Vaux, Charles L. Haight, Rotch & Tilden, and McKim, Mead and White. He traveled abroad extensively between 1894 and 1896, enlarging upon his study of architecture under a Rotch fellowship. The Watch Hill cottages he designed in partnership with Tracy appear to have been designed while he was also working for McKim, Mead and White. Magonigle also collaborated with Henry W. Wilkinson on designs for an alumni hall at Cornell University (not built) and a courthouse in Brooklyn, N.Y. After 1903, Magonigle was in practice alone. He was a prolific architect, sculptor, and artist, winning several medals and design competitions.

Gitche Gumee (Seaview, The Dug-Out), 1895, 189

La Maritima (The Boulders, Arcadia), 189

Ninigret, 1899

Chapman and Frazer

Horace Southworth Frazer, Boston (ca.1865-1931)

Frazer attended Yale and the Massachusetts Institute of Technology (MIT), receiving his degree in 1885. Afterward he associated with the architectural firms Peabody and Stearns, and Longfellow, Alden and Harlow, before joining with John Chapman in 1892. Chapman died in 1895; however, Frazer kept the Chapman and Frazer name, concentrating on residential work. Many of his designs were published in the leading architectural journals of the day, including *Architectural Record, American Architect,* and *American Architect and Building News.* A great body of his suburban residential work exists in the Boston area, particularly at Brookline and Chestnut Hill, where over 67 houses by Frazer are extant. His Watch Hill designs progress stylistically from the shingled, gambrel-roofed "Modern Colonial" to the stuccoed English Arts and Crafts. These later cottages are similar to his suburban Brookline commissions.

Not shown is the *Memorial Building* of the Watch Hill Improvement Society, 1917.

Sunshine Cottage, 1898

Cloverly, 1900

Tredegar (Russula), 1900

Red Top, 1900

Meadholme, 1900

Ridgeleigh (Ridgeleigh, Far Look), 1902

Emerson

William Ralph Emerson, Boston (1833-1917)

Known as one of the principal architects of the Shingle Style, Emerson was not formally educated as a designer. A cousin of Ralph Waldo Emerson and a friend of artist and designer William Morris Hunt, he grew up in Boston and Maine, and apprenticed with Jonathan Preston, a highly-regarded Boston builder. Emerson's architectural practice focused on individual residences for notable clients, including a Cambridge house for William James; he is particularly well-known for the summer cottages he designed in the Shingle Style at developing summer colonies along Boston's North Shore and on the Maine coast and islands, including *Felsted* for Frederick Law Olmsted, Sr. on Deer Isle. His cottages are sensitively designed in harmony with features of the site, expressing themselves as one with their setting through the use of stone and shingled walls, usually with a bold or exposed coastal location. Emerson's Shingle Style work ranks with that of Peabody and Stearns and McKim, Mead and White as innovative stylistic expression. His short-lived period of experimentation and exuberance in the Shingle Style was in the 1870s and 1880s. The known Emerson Watch Hill commission in the late 1890s, *Minnebama*, conveys Emerson's movement into the more formal and conservative Colonial Revival idiom, away from the inventiveness of the Shingle Style.

Minnebama (Pinecroft, Tick-Tock House), 189

Greenleaf and Cobb

Albert Winslow Cobb, Springfield, Massachusetts (1868-1941)

Cobb was educated at Tufts and MIT. He trained in architecture with two noted Boston firms of the period, first with Peabody and Stearns and later with Shepley, Rhutan and Coolidge. He also worked with William Ralph Emerson. Afterward, he joined the prolific coastal Maine architect John Calvin Stevens in his Boston and Portland practice and collaborated on an influential Shingle Style pattern book of the time: *Examples of American Domestic Architecture* (see page 39). Published in 1889, this illustrated book, among others, helped to solidify the Shingle Style as the iconic style for seaside summer houses on the New England coast. Cobb and Stevens designed numerous Shingle Style summer cottages along the Maine coast. In the 1890s Cobb moved to Springfield to open an office with Luther Greenleaf. Cobb's single known Watch Hill commission, *Appleby*, is from this period, although at least one other cottage, *Sunnyside*, 1895 (page 24, dormer, top right), may be derived from his pattern book.

Appleby (Sunset View, Wasigan), 189

Lawrence

Warrington Lawrence, New York (1861-1938)

A native of Baltimore, Lawrence graduated from MIT and began his career in the offices of McKim, Mead and White, where undoubtedly he was inspired by the firm's early 20th-century refinement of the Colonial Revival style. Lawrence's designs reflect a more academic, formal, and "grand estate" approach to domestic seaside and country house designs than the Shingle Style could provide. His work at Seabright and Glen Ridge, New Jersey, reflect this developing taste. A near duplicate of his Watch Hill design for *Clarmar* exists at Glen Ridge.

Clarmar, 1931

Eyre

Wilson Eyre, Philadelphia (1858-1944)

Eyre was born in Florence, Italy, but raised in Newport, R.I. He attended college at MIT for only one year, departing for Philadelphia where he began work for James Peacock Sims in 1877, taking over the office on Sims' death in 1882. Eyre is credited by many as a founder of the Shingle Style and his best known work is in that style. He lectured at the University of Pennsylvania between 1890 and 1894 and was a founder of *House and Garden* magazine. In 1911 he formed a partnership with John Gilbert McIlvaine; it is their country house work in the early 20th century that drew acclaim, providing Eyre in 1917 with the Gold Medal of the Philadelphia chapter of the American Institute of Architects (AIA). Eyre's known Watch Hill design, *Channel Mark,* is in the Colonial Revival style, including a central Palladian window, but also featuring an off-center entry porch and doorway.

Channel Mark (Anchorage), 1914

Pope

John Russell Pope, New York (1874-1937)

Pope studied architecture at The City College of New York and Columbia's School of Mines, graduating in 1894. He won a scholarship to the American Academy in Rome in 1895, spending an additional year traveling in Italy and Greece. He attended the Ecole des Beaux-Arts in 1896, opening his New York-based architectural practice in 1903. Pope became a premier designer in the popular styles of the early 20th century, notably the Tudor, 18th-century French, Georgian, and Beaux-Arts Classical Revival styles. In 1919 he created a master plan for Yale, and, several years later, one for Dartmouth (1922-23). He is particularly celebrated for his two large public commissions: the National Gallery of Art and the Jefferson Memorial, both built post-humously. His great Tudor houses include the Branch house in Richmond, Virginia (1917) and his own summer house, *The Waves*, in Newport, R.I. (1927). His Watch Hill commission, *The Timbers,* is a complex Tudor Revival estate consisting of a sprawling main house, gate lodge, and guest house with multi-level terraces situated on a knoll overlooking dunes and beach.

Schmidt

Mott B. Schmidt, New York (1889-1977)

Born in Middletown, N.Y., Schmidt studied architecture at the Pratt Institute, graduating in 1906. He then studied abroad for four years, and established his New York-based architectural practice in 1912. Through his association with Elsie deWolf, the pre-eminent American designer of fashionable interiors in the first decades of the 20th century, Schmidt gained several large commissions and became known as a "society architect," designing townhouses and country estates for Astors, Vanderbilts, and Rockefellers. His style reflected the taste for the revival styles of the early 20th century, including Tudor, Norman, Georgian, Classical Revival, and Mediterranean. His Watch Hill commissions are *Norman Hall* and *Windansea*.

The Timbers, 191

Windansea, 1922

Norman Hall (Stone House), 191

Landscape Architects & Their Work

Olmsted Brothers, Boston (1898-1961)

Founded by Frederick Law Olmsted, Sr. (1822-1903), who along with Calvert Vaux designed New York's Central Park (1858 et seq.), the noted Olmsted landscape architecture practice, by the late 1890s, was led by his sons, John Charles Olmsted (1852-1920) and Frederick Law Olmsted, Jr. (1870-1957). The legacy of this firm is legion with multiple commissions, both public and private across the country, spanning 100 years of work. Large-scale estate gardens were a specialty, along with planned residential communities, municipal park systems, and city master plans. Patrons included the most-celebrated Americans of the time. The Olmsteds also collaborated with the most-noted American architects of the period and trained in their office many of the period's finest landscape designers. Through their prodigious work, the Olmsteds, father, sons, and their associates, can be credited with establishing landscape architecture as a profession in America, bringing the need for urban parks and open space into the spotlight for livable cities during the mid-late 19th and early 20th centuries. Due to their enormous popularity, it is unusual that they appear to have had only a few commissions at Watch Hill, making the extant designed landscape features of these properties all the more interesting and important to preserve.

Not shown is *Sunny Hill (Ward House),* 1921.

Sunshine Cottage, garden, 1918, 1929

Misquamicut Club, 1919 clubhouse grounds, with a Donald Ross-designed Scottish links-style course added in 1923 (shown on page 32).

Warren Henry Manning, Boston (1860-1938)

Manning was among the last generation of self-educated landscape designers who began their work before landscape architecture became a profession. He trained with Frederick Law Olmsted, Sr. and was associated with Olmsted's firm for eight years from 1888-1896. Prior to this he worked with his father in their family's well-known nursery business in Reading, Massachusetts. Manning started his own design practice in 1896 and rapidly became successful with commissions for city park projects and estates, among the former, Wilcox Park in downtown Westerly. He was valued for his great knowledge of plant material and the environmental setting of his work. Along with Olmsted, Manning was a founding member of the American Society of Landscape Architects. He was also a faculty member at Harvard's Graduate School of Landscape Architecture. At Watch Hill, along with Robert F. Ballantine and Bradford Shinkle, the Clement A. Griscom family and their architect, Edward Foote Hinkle, were patrons, commissioning work for their cluster of summer cottages on Lighthouse Point and nearby Bluff Avenue.

Shown elsewhere are *Justholme (Seaesta, Weonit)*, 1905, page 35, upper left; *Hill House (The Kedge)*, 1903, page 31, lower right, and *The Point (The Manor House)*, 1906, page 42.

Trespasso, Seaswept, Moana

Moana (Aktaion), 190

Taurento, 190

Manning-designed landscapes on
Bluff Avenue and Lighthouse Point.

Wadley and Smythe, New York (1865-present)

Established in 1865, and located on Park Avenue at one time, Wadley and Smythe Florists provided both design and installation services on a large scale for society clients. Documented landscape commissions include the garden at *Arden House* (for Edward Henry Harriman) in Orange County, N.Y.; at *Wisteriahurst* (for William Skinner) in Holyoke Mass.; at *Avalon* (for Robert S. Brewster) in Mt. Kisco, N.Y.; and at *Vernon Court* (for Mrs. Richard Gambrill) in Newport, R.I. For some of these commissions they worked with well-known architects such as Delano and Aldrich, and Carrere and Hastings, both of New York. Whole landscapes were brought to their sites and installed. For example, the firm shipped plant material, trees, shrubs, and flowers in four box cars from New York to Louisville, Kentucky for installation of the garden at the Horace Trumbauer-designed Florence Brokaw Satterwhite memorial in 1928. The firm still exists today in its society florist, landscape design, and installation business as Irene Hayes Wadley & Smythe leMoult located at One Rockefeller Plaza.

Their known Watch Hill commission is *Sunset Hill.*

Sunset Hill, 1915

Marian Cruger Coffin, New York (1876-1957)

Coffin completed the landscape design program at MIT in 1904 and trained with Boston landscape designer Guy Lowell before opening her own practice in New York. She was one of the first women landscape architects to establish an office and a base of well-known patrons, including Henry Francis du Pont (at *Winterthur*), Childs Frick (at his estate in Roslyn, N.Y.), Edward F. Hutton and Marjorie Merriweather Post (at *Hillwood,* in Brookville, N.Y.), and Marshall Field (at *Caumsett,* in Lloyd Neck, N.Y.). These country house landscape and garden commissions are among the dozens of estate projects Coffin designed from the mid-Atlantic to New England. Coffin is also known for several municipal and institutional commissions, including the landscape of the University of Delaware, the New York Botanical Garden, and the harbor-front park in Watch Hill Village. Her design there included placement of Enid Yandell's bronze sculpture, "Chief Ningret," struck in Paris in 1911. Coffin maintained a summer home, *Wendover,* on East Hills Road in Watch Hill from 1921 until her death in 1957 and designed the small terrace garden there with defined outdoor rooms.

Not shown is *Wendover (Araconda),* ca.1912, garden after 1921.

Watch Hill Village Park, 1936

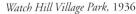

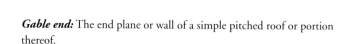

Glossary

Arts and Crafts movement: A late 19th- and early 20th-century stylistic trend in the decorative arts, furniture, and architecture, emphasizing simple and honest hand craftsmanship over machine-made products and a return to simpler, more refined forms without eclectic embellishment. The movement is often identified with Gustav Stickley, his periodical *The Craftsman*, and his furniture designs. Also known as the Craftsman Style in architecture.

Bargeboards: Also referred to as vergeboards, these are wide decorative trim boards accenting the roof line of a gable end.

Brackets: Decorative wood supports under roof eaves and soffits, usually L-shaped.

Colonial Revival: A stylistic period in the late 19th and early 20th centuries emphasizing American Colonial forms, but usually in a larger scale than the original. This trend was inaugurated with the popularity of the nation's centennial exposition in 1876, gaining momentum into the early-to-mid-20th century.

Eyebrow dormer: A form of arched window dormer expressed in a roof, popular in the Shingle Style and Colonial Revival periods.

Fanlight: A shallow, fan-shaped, arched window of multiple panes usually placed above a principal exterior door.

Gable end: The end plane or wall of a simple pitched roof or portion thereof.

Gable roof: A simple pitched roof of two intersecting planes.

Gambrel roof: A barn-like roof form popular with the American Colonial and Colonial Revival architectural styles consisting of four planes, the lower two planes being generally steeper than the upper two.

Gothic Revival: A romantic Victorian architectural and decorative arts style emphasizing European gothic forms. Arched windows and doorways, steeply pitched gable roofs, and other elements from medieval buildings are used for domestic, commercial, and institutional buildings.

Half-timbered: The exposed timber wood-frame system of Tudor houses, often with intervening spaces stuccoed or filled with brick work.

High Victorian Gothic: An interpretation of the Gothic Revival style, but emphasizing polychrome materials and banding, particularly in brick-work on wall planes and with slate or wood shingles on roofs. Often vertical elements and artful patterns are emphasized following the design philosophy of John Ruskin, a 19th-century British art critic, among others.

Hipped roof: A roof form popular in the American Colonial and Arts and Crafts movement where four shallow roof planes from each side of a building intersect in a ridge.

Mansard roof: A French roof form adopted in American architecture after the Civil War, where the primary roof plane is nearly the same angle as the wall below, allowing for an attic floor of greater volume than a conventional roof. Often this plane is curved. The upper portions of the roof are generally hipped in a shallow span to cover the building.

Mullion: A vertical dividing wall member between whole window sash units.

Muntin: A narrow wood or metal bar dividing window panes, to which the window panes are attached, within a movable or fixed window sash.

Porte-cochere: A deep porch extending from a driveway edge to an entrance or extended porch providing shelter to people and vehicles.

Potager: A kitchen garden combining vegetables, herbs, and flowers in an artful and mutually beneficial way; often fenced.

Queen Anne Style: A late 19th-century romantic architectural style derived from early American Colonial or post-medieval (late 17th century and early 18th century) forms such as high gables, broken pediments, and bay windows, and often embellished with turrets or towers and spreading porches. Decorative shingles and panels ornament gable ends and upper floors while lower floors are clapboard-clad or brick. This style is also referred to as "Free Classical." In plan, often there is a large central "living hall," with a staircase and inglenook fireplace, from which the other rooms open freely through wide archways.

Rhythm: The repetitive frequency, uniform size, and vertical alignment of window and door openings in a building's facade.

Shingle Style: A popular late 19th-century American seaside architectural style derived from the Queen Anne Style with extensive use of exterior shingle siding stretched across wall planes, corners, bays, soffits, and roofs. Roofs often conceal second and third floors and sweep down to cover porches or upper balconies.

Sidelights: Vertical window panels, generally narrow, that frame doorways.

Soffit: The paneled underside facing of a roof eave.

Surround: The ornamental work or decorative trim surrounding a door, window or fireplace opening.

Tudor Revival: An early 20th-century academic revival architectural style which captures the English medieval period of half-timbered buildings. This style is sometimes referred to as Elizabethan. Features include diagonal window muntins, diamond-shaped window panes, leaded glazing, and heavy exposed timbers (particularly in gable ends), which may be structural or applied. The spaces between the timbers may be stuccoed or bricked in.

Tuscan column: A simple round column post usually used for porch supports on late 19th-century Shingle Style houses. These are ornamented with simple capitals (or tops) and moldings in the "Roman" Doric order.

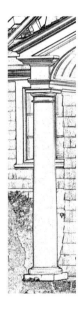

References with Select Annotations

Abbott, Steven. "John Calvin Stevens: The Early Years." In *Maine Home & Design*. Portland: Thomas Reid Publishing LLC, September, 2007.
    A review of the Shingle Style design work of architects John Calvin Stevens and Albert Winslow Cobb.

Aslet, Clive. *The American Country House.* New Haven: Yale University Press, 1990.
    A review of the movement and taste of country house-building with a section on the seaside.

Barnes, Chaplin Bradford. *Watch Hill Through Time: The Evolution of a New England Shore Community.* Watch Hill: The Watch Hill Conservancy, 2005.
    The story of Watch Hill, geologically and ecologically, from the Ice Age, and, in terms of human history, from aboriginal settlement to the present. A particular focus is on the development and social history of the community, from its heyday as a hotel resort destination to its transformation into a "cottage colony." Detailed information is provided about the cottages (with maps as to their location) and biographical sketches of many of their owners.

Birnbaum, Charles A. and Robin Karson, eds. *Pioneers of American Landscape Design: An Annotated Bibliography.* New York: McGraw-Hill Education, 2000.

Cutler, Laurence. "Gardens at Vernon Court to be open for ...." In *Musenews.* Newport: The National Museum of American Illustration, April 6, 2006.
    The Wadley and Smythe landscape design firm is described with regard to the restoration of their design at *Vernon Court* in Newport, R.I.

Dray, Eric, and Gretchen Schuler. *Westerly Preservation Report 2006.* Westerly: Westerly Preservation Society, 2006.
    This report synthesizes the state of preservation of each of Westerly's National Register-listed Historic Districts, and others eligible for listing, with recommendations for protection.

Embury, Aymar II. *One Hundred Country Houses: Modern American Examples.* New York: The Century Co., 1909.
    A period coffee table book of black and white pictures of houses classified as to style. Grosvenor Atterbury, among others, is featured.

Gabriel, Cleota Reed. *The Arts & Crafts Ideal: The Ward House, An Architect & his Craftsmen.* Syracuse: The Institute for Development of Evolutive Architecture, Inc., 1978.
    An exhibit catalogue of the work of architect Ward Wellington Ward and the Syracuse, N.Y. center for the Arts and Crafts movement of which Watch Hill architect Henry Wilhelm Wilkinson was an early influential member.

"George Keller." At www.bushnellpark.org, the web site of the Bushnell Park Foundation, 2009.
    Information on architect George Keller and his work in Hartford.

Gray, Christopher. "Streetscapes/Harperly Hall: Restoring an Arts and Crafts Co-op Masterpiece." In *The New York Times,* Real Estate section. New York: November 13, 1994.
    Description of a well-known Henry Wilhelm Wilkinson design in New York City.

Griswold, Mac and Eleanor Weller. *The Golden Age of American Gardens: Proud Owners, Private Estates, 1890-1940.* New York: Harry N. Abrams, Inc., 2000.
    Information on the work of landscape architects the Olmsted Brothers, Warren Manning, and Marian Cruger Coffin, among many others.

Hewitt, Mark Alan. *The Architecture of Mott B. Schmidt.* New York: Rizzoli, 1991.

Holmes, Deborah. "Victorian Shingle Style Houses, 1880-1900." At www.oldhouseweb.com, the web site of the Old House Web, 2008.

Jordy, William H. and Christopher Monkhouse. *Buildings on Paper: Rhode Island Architectural Drawings, 1825-1945.* Providence: Bell Art Gallery, Brown University; Rhode Island Historical Society; and Museum of Art, Rhode Island School of Design, 1982.
    An extensive catalogue of design work in Rhode Island, including biographies of architects.

Jordy, William H. and Ronald J. Onorato, William McKenzie Woodward, contributing editors. *Buildings of Rhode Island.* New York: Oxford University Press, 2004.
    An extensive catalogue of buildings in Rhode Island, including Watch Hill.

Lang, Derryl G. "The Development of a Summer Resort: Watch Hill, Rhode Island." Master's Thesis. Graduate School of Architecture, Planning, and Preservation, Columbia University, 1988.
> A history of the development of Watch Hill from a social, planning, and architectural perspective.

National Register of Historic Places: Watch Hill, Rhode Island, Watch Hill Historic District. Prepared by Robert O. Jones, Jr. (RIHPC, 1985). Watch Hill: The Watch Hill Preservation Society, 1988.
> Includes a section on historical significance and sections describing the houses of Watch Hill with a building list by street address. (Some street names have since changed.)

"Olmsted Research Guide Online." At www.rediscov.com/olmsted/, the research guide web site of the Frederick Law Olmsted National Historic Site.

Ransom, David F. *George Keller, Architect.* Hartford: The Stowe-Day Foundation, 1978.

Reid, Roger, ed. *Establishment of Chestnut Hill North Local Historic District.* A Report Prepared by the Chestnut Hill Neighborhood Association. Brookline, Mass.: Brookline Preservation Commission and Department of Planning and Community Development, February 8, 2005.
> Many dwellings in the district were designed by architect Horace Southworth Frazer. They are catalogued by street and described. Some are very similar to those he designed at Watch Hill.

Schneider, Ardith, Roberta M. Burkhardt and Michael Beddard. *Watch Hill Then & Now.* Watch Hill: The Watch Hill Preservation Society, 2005 (revised 2008).
> A large-format book with many black and white historical and current photos of Watch Hill cottages. Nearly every cottage is depicted.

Scully, Vincent J. *The Shingle Style and the Stick Style, revised edition: Architectural Theory and Design from Downing to the Origins of Wright.* New Haven: Yale University Press, 1973.
> Break-through analysis and identification of the genre.

Smithsonian Institution Research Information System (SIRIS), Washington, DC, 2009.
> Information is provided on architects and their work.

Society of Architectural Historians. "American Architects' Biographies." At www.sah.org, the web site of the Society of Architectural Historians, 2009.

Sterngass, Jon. *First Resorts: Pursuing Pleasure at Saratoga Springs, Newport & Coney Island.* Baltimore: The Johns Hopkins University Press, 2001.
> An analysis of post-Civil War summer resort popularity and life.

Stevens, John Calvin, and Albert Winslow Cobb. *Examples of American Domestic Architecture,* New York, 1889.
> A period architectural pattern book with illustrations of Shingle Style New England seaside summer cottages, some of which bear resemblance to several Watch Hill cottages.

Stickley, Gustav. *Craftsman Homes: Architecture and Furnishings of the American Arts & Crafts Movement* (reproduction of the 1909 edition). New York: Dover Publications, 1979.

Vadney, Greg. "Wilkinson helped create 'New Furniture' design." At www.syracuse.com, the web site of the publication *Syracuse,* October 23, 2008.
> Article on architect Henry Wilhelm Wilkinson as one of Gustav Stickley's early collaborators on furniture design.

Walker, Sam, ed. *American Gardens.* New York: Acanthus Press, 2006.

"Warren Manning Project." At www.lalh.org, the web site of the Library of American Landscape History, 2009.
> A research and documentation project of landscape architect Warren Manning's work, which documents, in part, his work at Watch Hill.

Withey, Henry F. and Elise R. *Biographical Dictionary of American Architects (Deceased).* Los Angeles: Henessey and Ingalls, 1956.
> A respected source for architects' biographies.

Woodward, William McKenzie. *Historic Landscapes of Rhode Island.* Providence: The Rhode Island Historical Preservation & Heritage Commission, 2001.
> A survey of Watch Hill landscapes is included, with biographical sketches of the designers, including the Olmsted Brothers, Warren Manning, and Marian Cruger Coffin.

Zaitzevsky, Cynthia. *The Architecture of William Ralph Emerson, 1833-1917: Catalogue.* Cambridge, Mass: Harvard University Press, 1969.